Gluten-Eating

Guide to Starting and Sticking to a Gluten-Free Lifestyle so You Can Take Your Health and Wellbeing to a Whole New Level

By Paul Dillow

© **Copyright 2020 - All rights reserved.**

The content contained within this book may not be reproduced, duplicated or transmitted without direct written permission from the author or the publisher.

Under no circumstances will any blame or legal responsibility be held against the publisher or author for any damages, reparation, or monetary loss due to the information contained within this book. Either directly or indirectly.

Legal Notice:

This book is copyright protected. This book is only for personal use. You cannot amend, distribute, sell, use, quote or paraphrase any part, or the content within this book, without the consent of the author or publisher.

Disclaimer Notice:

Please note the information contained within this document is for educational and entertainment purposes only. All effort has been executed to present accurate, up to date and reliable, complete information. No warranties of any kind are declared or implied. Readers acknowledge that the author is not engaging in the rendering of legal, financial, medical or professional advice. The content within this book has been derived from various sources. Please consult a licensed professional before attempting any techniques outlined in this book.

By reading this document, the reader agrees that under no circumstances is the author responsible for any losses, direct or indirect, which are incurred as a result of the use of information contained within this document, including, but not limited to, —errors, omissions, or inaccuracies.

Contents

Introduction 1

Chapter 1-- What is Gluten? 4

Chapter 2—Why All the Fuss? 8

    1. Celiac Disease 8

    2. Gluten Sensitivity 10

    3. Gluten Intolerance 11

Chapter 3-- How to Diagnose Gluten Sensitivity, Celiac Disease and Gluten Intolerance 13

    Celiac Disease Diagnosis 14

    Diagnosing Gluten Intolerance or Gluten Sensitivity 15

    Drawbacks of the Medical System 15

Chapter 4-- How to Make it Easier for Your Physician to Make a Diagnosis 17

    Keep a Food Journal 17

    Write Down Your Signs 18

    Inform your Physician of Other Medical Conditions 20

    Inform your Physician of the Medical History of Your Family 21

    Be on Time For Your Session 21

    Have Patience 22

Chapter 5-- What are the Good Things About Gluten-Free Life? 24

Chapter 6-- Risks of Gluten-Free Eating 30

Chapter 7-- How to Delight In Gluten-Free Eating 36

Chapter 8-- So ... What Should You Eat 41

Chapter 9-- Simple Gluten-Free Options 46

Conclusion 50

Thank you for buying this book and I hope that you will find it useful. If you will want to share your thoughts on this book, you can do so by leaving a review on the Amazon page, it helps me out a lot.

Introduction

You choosing to read this book is proof that the Gluten-Free movement is gradually increasing in appeal. Individuals all over the world have actually made a decision that staying clear of gluten was not simply another diet alternative, but something that is vital to their health. This is not simply another trend that is going to lose momentum before you get time to even investigate it, and it is definitely not another insane fad diet.

This shift has actually been deemed as the most sensible method for plenty of individuals to shed pounds, take charge of their health, and begin feeling like themselves once again. However, make no mistake, this diet is not for everybody. Adhering to a Gluten-Free diet is going to lead you down a road that is certainly wrought with hardship.

The issue lies in the truth that gluten is all over! Attempting to get rid of a component that is featured in such a broad range of foods is bound to be difficult. The very first hurdle is going to be discovering the self-discipline to stop eating a fair bit of the food you have actually grown to enjoy. This sounds a lot easier than it is when the 'healthier' alternative is not as yummy. The next difficulty is going to be discovering how to get adequate quantities of the nutrients you require to remain healthy without jeopardizing your decision to stay clear of gluten. And if that wasn't enough, the majority of the foods classified as "Gluten-Free" might be more pricey than their equivalents.

Whatever you choose, constantly keep in mind that your body is your home. If you do not make an effort to look after it, where are you going to live? Making an effort to eat right, exercise, and get enough rest are going to constantly be good choices. Executing effectively and at the highest level of your efficiency are going to just be possible if you look after yourself. This may need a bit more time and a little bit more effort, however, it is going to definitely be worth it.

Regrettably, there is no 'one size fits all' when it concerns our wellness and health. You need to put in the work yourself and examine your own distinct requirements. You are never ever going to have the ability to pour from an empty cup. So trust me, spend some time learning what your bodily requirements are.

By now, you ought to be questioning if all the hassle is truly worth it. And once again, I urge you to think thoroughly about whether this diet plan is actually appropriate for you. This diet plan might not be quite what you require. If it is, nevertheless, the advantages are going to far surpass any difficulties you deal with as a result of going down this path. I hate to sound sensational, however cutting gluten from your diet plan might even save your life. In order for you to be certain that this diet plan is appropriate for you, please keep on reading on to find out more about gluten and why staying clear of it is such a biggie. This might very well wind up being among the most important decisions you have actually ever made.

Chapter 1-- What is Gluten?

Simply put, gluten is among the proteins discovered in cereal grains like rye, wheat and barley. Gluten is made by a mix of 2 various proteins. These proteins are Glutenin and Gliadin. The plant depends on its supply of gluten due to the fact that it works as food for the plant throughout growth. When these grains are ground into flour, the gluten is in charge of the elasticity of dough mixes.

It is this flexibility that offers our food a particular "chewiness." People who struggle with Gluten intolerance are frequently urged to stay clear of oats too. This is since oats can quickly be tainted by foods that contain gluten, considering that it is typically processed in factories that produce food utilizing wheat and other foods that contain gluten. Some instances of gluten-free grains are sorghum, millet, buckwheat, brown rice, quinoa, wild rice, and corn.

Wheat is frequently utilized to make the following foods:

- Pasta

- Bread

- Sauces

- Baked goods

- Soups

- Cakes

- Battered meat, fish and poultry

- Salad dressings

Rye is utilized to make foods like:

- Cereals

- Pumpernickel bread

- Beer

Barley is frequently utilized to make:

- Food coloring
- Beer
- Malt milk
- Yeast
- Soups
- Malt vinegar

A lot of the foods we consume might additionally consist of some quantity of gluten as a result of being polluted throughout the manufacturing procedure. These foods consist of:

- Candy
- Dried fruit
- Caramel color
- Flavored coffee
- French fries
- Food starch

- Vegetable and meat stock

- Processed meats and cheese

- Dietary Supplements like multivitamins

- Bouillon cubes

- Ice cream

This list is not comprehensive. Time is not going to allow me to note all the foods which have or don't have gluten, and even if I had the time, you would deem it rather dull. The only effective means to figure out if your food includes gluten is to read the label thoroughly. This is going to need a great deal of your time in order for you to be precise. This comprehensive procedure might not be right for everybody.

Chapter 2—Why All the Fuss?

A current study highlighted that about 30% of all Americans are actively attempting to remove gluten from their diet plan. This are plenty of individuals when we consider the reality that there are over 330,000,000 individuals in the United States. However, why are they making such a fuss? Let's take a look at a few of the reasons why many individuals have actually chosen to live Gluten Free.

1. Celiac Disease

Research studies have actually shown that the number of people who presently struggle with this disease is on the increase. Although no official numbers have actually been released, it is approximated that well over 1% of the world's population experiences this disease. Celiac disease is specifically prevalent amongst the senior people. Even worse is the reality that lots of cases of people who struggle with this disease have actually gone undiagnosed. Actually, about 80% of individuals who struggle with celiac disease are not even cognizant that they have it.

However, exactly what is celiac disease you may be asking yourself? As emphasized in the last chapter, gluten is made up of 2 primary proteins, Glutenin and Gliadin. People with Celiac Disease react adversely to Gliadin. Celiac is categorized as an autoimmune illness. That is due to the fact that the immune system of these people tends to confuse gluten with something unsafe like a bacteria of some kind. Consequently, their bodies attempt to protect themselves from the gluten and wind up hurting themselves while doing so. This attack can lead to the degeneration of the intestinal wall and could be dangerous if not dealt with.

Other signs of Celiac Disease consist of:

- Anemia

- Nutritional shortages

- Throwing up

- Chronic fatigue

- Abdominal pain

- Abdominal bloating

- Digestive problems

- Diarrhea

- Scratchy skin rashes

- Reduced hunger

- Depression

- Irritability

- Damaged tooth enamel

- Osteoporosis

- Heartburn

- Joint pain

2. Gluten Sensitivity

Others, who do not experience Celiac Disease, have actually decided to stay clear of gluten or cut it out of their diet plan completely due to the fact that they struggle with Gluten Sensitivity. These people might have even gotten a negative result when they undertook a blood test for celiac, however, you just do not feel good when they take in foods which contain gluten. They might even struggle with signs that are rather comparable to those of somebody who has celiac disease.

Struggling With gluten sensitivity indicates that the person responds adversely to gluten despite the fact that their immune system is not harming their bodies. The signs of gluten sensitivity are normally unrelated to the intestinal tract, and they don't induce any damage to the intestinal tracts whatsoever. On the contrary, these people are more likely to experience joint pain, tiredness, abdominal pain, and even 'brain fog.' The good news is that gluten sensitivity is not deadly.

3. Gluten Intolerance

Gluten intolerance is additionally not deadly. It is going to, nevertheless, induce a fair bit of pain. People with this condition can not digest or process foods which contains gluten. This could be for a range of reasons. That person's body might not be able to produce the enzyme required to digest foods which contain gluten. Signs of gluten intolerance are generally digestion associated and might consist of bloating, gas, nausea, or diarrhea. Simply consider the outcome of eating dairy when you're lactose intolerant.

You ought to now have the understanding that living gluten-free is a really major matter for some people, and it is not a decision to be sneezed at. You are going to have the ability to value the severity of the matter, specifically if you experience these signs also. Chapter 3 of this book is about figuring out if you have any of the major gluten associated conditions that have actually been pointed out.

Chapter 3-- How to Diagnose Gluten Sensitivity, Celiac Disease and Gluten Intolerance

The significant problem with identifying whether you have gluten sensitivity, celiac disease, or gluten intolerance is that the signs look a lot like those you would have if you struggled with other illnesses. And since gluten is present in such a wide array of foods, it is simple to confuse these problems with your body merely responding adversely to a specific kind of food. That is why I would never ever urge anybody to attempt and diagnose themselves. Celiac disease can be deadly if left unattended and if the proper actions are not taken to minimize its impacts.

Although gluten intolerance and sensitivity are not deadly conditions, neglecting the signs can induce damage to your body over time. Leave the testing to the specialists. Consider how harmful it would be if you 'under-diagnosed' yourself as being gluten-sensitive when you really have celiac disease. Despite the fact that you are going to be leaving the last medical diagnosis to the specialists, it still would not hurt to find out more about the procedure.

Celiac Disease Diagnosis

A blood test is frequently utilized to validate whether your signs are due to celiac disease. Keep in mind That celiac disease happens when your body confounds the protein in gluten called Gliadin as a hazardous compound and attacks it. Your immune system is created to generate a protein referred to as an antibody so as to eradicate any organism your body thinks to be harmful. This is additionally the case when you struggle with celiac disease.

Your body is going to produce particular antibodies so as to protect itself from gluten. Blood tests are, therefore, carried out to check if your body is generating the antibodies that are specific to combating gluten. Physicians typically check for high levels of the antibody referred to as Immunoglobulin A (IgA) anti-tissue transglutaminase.

Diagnosing Gluten Intolerance or Gluten Sensitivity

Among the simplest ways for physicians to figure out if you struggle with gluten intolerance or gluten sensitivity is to ask you to do away with gluten from your diet plan for a duration of approximately 1 month. If your signs vanish or end up being less considerable during the time you stay clear of gluten, and these signs come back when you reinstitute gluten into your diet plan, then it is apparent that your body is responding adversely to gluten. A blood test can additionally be utilized to figure out if you experience either one of these conditions.

Drawbacks of the Medical System

Gluten was not a huge deal 10 years back. Physicians are even more worried about enhancing their procedure for diagnosing Cancer and STDs. Far less time is committed to investigating negative reactions to consuming gluten. Consequently, even well-meaning physicians merely confuse the signs of gluten intolerance or celiac disease with another thing.

Screening for celiac disease is most likely going to be among the last things your physician is going to suggest. In addition, there has actually been a significant quantity of cases of Physicians under diagnosing their patients' signs. Chapter 4 of this book is going to discuss how you can assist your physician to precisely diagnose you.

Chapter 4-- How to Make it Easier for Your Physician to Make a Diagnosis

As emphasized in the prior chapter, your physician is not without fault. I am not urging you to mistrust any physician who has comprehensive training and years of experience. I am, nevertheless, urging you to lend them a hand. About 14% of all medical diagnoses are false. And regardless of the very best efforts of our hard-working physicians, this is additionally true when it comes to cases which entail an adverse response to gluten. The good news is, there is a lot you can do to assist your physician in making the very best diagnosis.

Here are my recommendations:

Keep a Food Journal

By now, it ought to be rather apparent that your signs relate to your diet plan. This is often the case when your signs relate to your intestinal system. Keeping a food journal demands that you monitor the foods you consume and how frequently you consume them. In an effort to be as precise as possible, I would additionally urge you to write down the amount in which you take in these foods.

This type of information is going to provide your physician with a clear idea of the kind of food which might or might not be triggering your signs. I would urge you to do this for about 2 weeks prior to your visit. This is going to spare you a lot of time due to the fact that the majority of physicians frequently advise that you keep a precise food journal prior to making a medical diagnosis.

Write Down Your Signs

Your physician may be understanding, however, they definitely can not actually feel your pain. They are not going to have the ability to make a precise medical diagnosis if they can not isolate your signs. That is why you have to help them comprehend what you are feeling. Documenting your signs is going to be a vital gift to your physician since it is going to assist him/her in dismissing a number of unassociated conditions in a matter of minutes. Prepare a list of all your signs and the frequency of their appearance. It would additionally be great to include whether these signs happen at a particular time, like when you are doing some kind of exercise.

Be as particular as possible. For instance, please do not tell your physician that your stomach is in pain. Where does it hurt? Is it in your lower abdominal area? Is the pain acute? How long does the discomfort last? Expect the type of questions your physician is going to have to ask and write down the answers to the questions as specifically as possible. Offering this sort of information is going to spare both you and your physician a great deal of time.

In some cases, it is when we point out one particular sign or series of signs that assist the physician in piecing together the puzzle of your disease. And isn't it true that we often forget to state a few of our signs to our physicians? This is going to guarantee you say all that you have to say without needing to spend the entire day with your physician.

Inform your Physician of Other Medical Conditions

If you experience other health problems, you might have signs that might lead your physician to make an inaccurate medical diagnosis. Providing him/her with the clearest understanding of your present medical status is the very best method to assist him or her in making the very best medical diagnosis. You are going to additionally assist your physician not to squander time looking into treatments for a condition for which you have actually already gotten medication. Providing your physician with a list of your existing medications is additionally a great idea. That is going to guarantee that your physician does not recommend something that is not going to mix with your present medication.

Your physician might have to change your existing medication in order to deal with whatever brand-new condition he has actually determined. Your physician might additionally have to advise some changes to your diet plan if gluten is, in fact, impacting you adversely. He/she is going to have to have a clear image of how changing your diet plan is going to impact how your body responds to your existing medication and make the very best suggestion.

Inform your Physician of the Medical History of Your Family

Your household's medical history acts as a map to your own medical status. You are fairly likely to struggle with conditions that prevail amongst your family members. This is specifically accurate when it comes to your moms and dads who have the greatest impact on your health. Do not hesitate to ask. Our family members, specifically the males, might want to appear strong in our eyes; however, finding out about their health problems can save you.

Be on Time For Your Session

Although this is a little unrelated, I believe it has to be stated that we are frequently not too mindful of our physician's time. Appearing for a session late is going to put your physician in an extremely uncomfortable position. They are going to either need to force you to wait or infringe on the time of another individual. In either case, this is an extremely inconsiderate act and you should do your best not to place your physician in such a position.

We are all really busy individuals, however, intentionally squandering the time of individuals responsible for saving lives is rather reprehensible. If you need to be late because of some inescapable disaster, I highly urge you to call the physician's office and notify them as early as possible. This is going to give them ample time to thoroughly reorganize their schedule so as to accommodate other individuals who might be waiting. The physician might even have the ability to utilize this time to take a well required and definitely, a well-deserved break.

Have Patience

Awaiting a medical diagnosis might appear to take forever. Some have actually even portrayed it as the longest wait of their lives. The minutes, hours, and even days that might go by might be painful, however, please remain patient. Bugging your physician is going to get you nowhere fast. Some things, such as the queue of blood samples waiting to be evaluated at the laboratory, are merely out of your physician's control. Enable them peace of mind and the time required to reach the most precise conclusion.

So far, we have actually explored what gluten is, how it adversely impacts some people, and even how to determine if it is damaging you. Next, we are going to turn our focus to the advantages of staying with a gluten-free diet plan.

Chapter 5-- What are the Good Things About Gluten-Free Life?

It goes without stating that eating a Gluten-Free diet plan is going to be extremely beneficial to those people who experience the gluten-associated diseases pointed out in the previous chapters. For some, this may be as easy as staying clear of stomach pain or those scratchy bumps or as significant as saving your life. Whatever the case might be, the advantages are going to speak for themselves. However, eating Gluten-free goes far beyond assisting us in staying clear of whatever signs we might have when we eat gluten. Let us take a look at these benefits from another viewpoint.

First of all, cutting gluten from your diet plan is going to push you to pay really careful attention to the foods you have actually been consuming. As soon as somebody chooses to stay clear of gluten at all costs, they are going to have to begin looking at labels and asking relevant questions.

As pointed out in chapter 1, it is simple to recognize the foods which clearly include gluten, like bread, however, how are you going to know if your dried fruits have been sprayed with a component which contains wheat in order to enhance the taste? Do you believe that grocery store attendants and restaurant owners are going to hurry to your side when they believe you will eat or buy something which contains gluten? Do you believe they want you to stop purchasing their items?

Obviously not! Your life remains in danger, so you have to step up and take all the required safety measures. When you start to inspect the labels of the foods you consume a bit more vigilantly, you are going to start to see how dreadful certain components in our foods are. Some foods include synthetic flavors, hazardous preservatives, and chemicals you would rather not take in. You are going to be stunned to see that gluten is not the only villain in your food. These hazardous ingredients are typically carcinogenic and can result in major damage to our bodies with time. These stunning discoveries are going to drive you to look for natural options, and therein lays another advantage of the gluten-free diet plan.

The very best option for this kind of diet plan is to stay clear of excessively processed foods. A lot of pastas and bread, for instance, are created with bleached wheat and other harmful compounds. A number of the gluten-free alternatives are going to be created from other, more wholesome whole grains that have actually been processed only enough for the food to be pleasurable, however, not excessively so that they have actually protected as much of the nutrients in the food as feasible.

Extremely processed foods are additionally infamous for consisting of unhealthy oils too. Hence, a gluten-free diet plan, when given careful consideration, is going to assist you to additionally stay clear of the host of diseases connected with consuming excessive, extremely processed carbs and oils.

Numerous people who have actually chosen to stay with a gluten-free diet plan have actually found themselves consuming even more fresh vegetables and fruits than they would have taken in had they not been on this particular diet plan. A diet plan abundant in an assortment of healthy foods is constantly one that comes strongly suggested.

Taking in more vegetables and fruits is going to assist in reinforcing your immune system and offering you an amazing quantity of energy to deal with every day. Taking in a diet plan this wholesome is going to additionally assist you in keeping a healthy body weight if you additionally put in the time to get routine exercise and enough rest.

Individuals who are brand-new to a specific diet plan, frequently grumble that they deal with most difficulties and temptations when they choose to eat in restaurants. Usually, the waiter is uninformed or too occupied to describe whether your meal is going to include gluten. Furthermore, cross-contamination is a really strong possibility in these circumstances and can pose a major danger, particularly to those with celiac disease.

These problems end up being a lot more troublesome when you are eating in a group. You do not wish to seem like the weird one, and you definitely do not wish to piss off the waiter that is going to be serving your food. Due to these obstacles, numerous gluten-free zealots have actually decided to eat in restaurants less. Eating in your home regularly is going to provide these people with complete control over what they consume. You now have the choice to make tasty meals that are going to have no irritating side effects. I am not urging you to be antisocial, I am just describing what has actually worked for other folks who are in our shoes. Plus, consuming home-cooked meals is going to be good for you in many ways.

Advantages of eating at home:

- Places you in control of the portion sizes of your food

- Saves Cash

- You can feel confident that your food is prepped in a sanitary environment

- Exceptional possibilities for family bonding while the food is being prepped and eaten

There is additionally some cutting-edge research that is presently happening, which highlights that there is a connection between eating gluten-free and autism. Research studies have actually demonstrated that eating gluten-free has actually reduced the signs of autism for some kids. There is still a great deal of clashing reviews about the findings of research of this kind. It is, nevertheless, rather notable, that lots of kids' hospitals have actually reported seeing an enhancement in the social skills and behavior of kids with autism who have actually been moved to a gluten-free diet plan.

There is no question in my mind that eating gluten-free is a terrific idea if you experience any gluten-associated condition. Ideally, you too are going to be persuaded that this is an excellent idea for yourself. Please nevertheless pay close attention to the next chapter of this book due to the fact that, just like any choice, there are drawbacks when it comes to cutting gluten from your diet plan too.

Chapter 6-- Risks of Gluten-Free Eating

Among the significant problems with starting the journey of a gluten-free diet plan is that lots of people who start this journey just do not comprehend what they are entering into. They merely dive headfirst into this choice, believing it is simply another weight loss diet trend or another healthy diet plan alternative. While the advantages of this diet plan are apparent, you have to thoroughly evaluate whether this is appropriate for you. Even if you struggle with a properly diagnosed gluten-associated health problem, ample forethought ought to be given to what you do next.

2 of the risks connected with not thoroughly planning your gluten-free program that are typically highlighted are:

1. Losing out on important nutrients

2. Taking in unhealthy gluten-free foods

People who have actually chosen to take part in the gluten-free program for whatever reason without thoroughly considering their alternatives, frequently wind up losing out on essential nutrients. In spite of whatever medical conditions or goals you might have about your perfect body, health ought to constantly be our primary focus. It is inconceivable to stay healthy without a well-balanced diet plan.

A person has a well-balanced diet plan when they make an effort to take in the advised quantity of the vital nutrients our bodies require daily. Taking in an excessive or insufficient amount of any one nutrient is not going to serve to your benefit in the long run, even if you accomplish the objective of losing some excess weight.

The danger of winding up lacking in particular nutrients ends up being really genuine to those who adhere to a gluten-free diet plan due to the fact that they have actually considerably cut down on their choices. Gluten is featured in such a wide array of foods that removing it from your diet plan is going to need a lot of changes. Plenty of those who venture to stay clear of gluten are really busy individuals and have lots of clashing obligations.

This hectic world needs rather a great deal of our time, and we frequently need to sacrifice sleep simply to get all the things done. Consuming a nutritious diet plan was already really hard, and now you have actually chosen to additionally complicate your regimen by choosing to live gluten-free.

The outcome of this mix of having an excessive amount of things to do, and very few choices is going to lead to one of these 3 things. The person might wind up consuming a great deal of 'gluten-free fast foods.' They might additionally wind up just eating the identical things repeatedly. They might additionally wind up simply giving up entirely. If you started this journey since you struggle with celiac disease or another gluten-associated condition, stopping is simply not a possibility. You need to discover an approach to make this diet plan work for the benefit of your health, and in some cases, even your life.

Sadly, the other alternatives that I pointed out weren't such great ideas either. Consuming identical things repeatedly is going to suggest that you are taking in the identical nutrients constantly. This type of uniformity is going to make sticking to this diet plan extremely tough since you aren't going to delight in eating the identical thing so frequently. Consuming the identical foods constantly might not seem like such a bad thing, however, simply think of the nutrients that you are missing out on when you eat in such a manner.

In some cases, it is that one nutrient that is missing from our diet plan that makes the distinction in your health. For instance, a number of gluten-free bread alternatives frequently utilize alternatives to wheat, which include far less dietary fiber. Dietary supplements may assist in reducing the impacts of those sorts of eating practices, however, this is never ever the best choice. It is going to take some amount of preparation on your part to get the appropriate mix of nutrients.

Another significant obstacle numerous people deal with due to choosing to live gluten-free is that they end up being puzzled about the type of foods that are really beneficial to their health. Since this movement is getting momentum, sly marketing execs have actually been tagging many things as gluten-free. I have even noticed gluten-free labels on bottles of water. Sending out such a hoodwinking of a message can just serve to hurt the customers.

To make matters worse, a great deal of the foods which are being offered as Gluten-free are, in fact, really bad for your health. So as to make these foods tastier, the manufacturers frequently add a great deal of sugar or fat. A great deal of these gluten-free foods are frequently over-processed too. That is why I can not stress enough how essential it is for you to read the labels of all the things you consume. Inspect the calorie, sugar and fat content of each product. Do not make the error of presuming these products benefit your health just as long as they are tagged 'gluten-free.' As highlighted in a previous chapter, you need to watch out for your own best interest. These sly suppliers frequently do not have your best interest in mind.

This information isn't made to terrify you. However, your health is a very severe matter. If you are not cautious, your life may be at stake. You can never

ever be too cautious with what you take into your body. Take the utmost precaution with anything you mean to consume, regardless of how healthy it may seem. Put in the time to do some investigation on anything brand-new or that may appear suspicious. When in doubt, adhere to natural options. You can never ever fail with ground provisions, fresh fruits and veggies. However, it could be very hard to find out how to delight in consuming healthy foods. That is why the last chapter is going to offer you a couple of easy dishes to assist you in getting going.

Chapter 7-- How to Delight In Gluten-Free Eating

Consuming a Gluten-free diet plan does not need to be dull. As formerly highlighted, staying with any diet plan is going to end up being more troublesome if you push yourself to consume identical things repeatedly. This is not going to drive you to stay with your diet plan. And the minute you see anything that resembles a challenge, you are going to quit. Sadly, quitting is not a possibility if you have gluten sensitivity, celiac disease, or gluten intolerance. Your life and your health are in question, and you have to continue going.

Here are my recommendations to keep yourself encouraged to stay with this diet plan:

1. Mix it Up!

This is the primary step to delighting in your Gluten-free journey. Do not hesitate to attempt brand-new things. If in doubt, look at the label or do some research on the web. When you are sure it does not include any gluten, dig in! Integrate it into meals you currently take pleasure in. Mixing it up is going to additionally require that you attempt brand-new recipes. Your meals ought to resemble a masterpiece. This does not indicate they need to be fancy, they just have to be enticing to the eyes. Integrate a range of various colors, textures, and flavors. Do not be upset if you fall short a couple of times prior to getting it right. This is all part of the journey.

2. Do Not Cut the Carbs!

This may appear like a rational step to feature in any diet plan. That is, nevertheless, when you are making the error of presuming that gluten-free diet plan is similar to any other diet plan. Constantly bear in mind that your objective is merely to stay clear of foods with gluten. Carbohydrates are not the enemy. As soon as you have actually done your homework to identify if the food is safe, dig in.

3. Treat Yourself

I additionally highly suggest that you treat yourself every so often. This is another method to stay clear of making this diet plan feel difficult or uninteresting. Gluten-free treats are rather simple to discover and are just as satisfying. Now that your choices are a bit more restricted, you may additionally wish to think about different nuts and fruits as a reward. Yogurt treats and dried fruits, for instance, are simply magnificent, and there are a lot more choices to select from. You may even have choices like these as routine treats in between meals.

4. Do not Starve Yourself!

This brand-new diet plan is not going to require that you consume less calories daily. Please do not starve yourself. You may even discover yourself taking in a bit more. Some Gluten-free options, particularly those created from natural components, frequently include a lot less calories than we are used to. The outcome is that we are going to have to consume a bit more of these kinds of food in order to be pleased. Once more, there is no shame in that when you have actually performed the needed research to figure out that this food is harmless.

5. Do not be Shy!

There is no requirement to be timid about eating gluten-free. Speak out and inform your loved ones, buddies, and even the waiter serving you that you have actually picked this diet plan and describe the severity of your choice. Once they comprehend the gravity of the scenario, they too are going to end up being rather alert and assist you in keeping track of the foods you consume too. They are going to have your back and function as an additional set of eyes too.

Keep in mind, 2 heads are much better than one. And believe me, it is constantly much better to simply speak the fact than to attempt and conceal your decision or your health problem. You are going to appear quite odd when you begin staying away from the foods you once liked. Your buddies may even end up being a little concerned and presume you are on some unsafe fad diet. Calmly describing the reasoning behind it all is going to get their assistance and trust.

What you ought to take away from this chapter is that living gluten-free could be amazing and fun. Think about it as a tough brand-new food journey. You are going to be boldly moving outside your comfort zone and delving into uncharted territory. Some have actually even explained dieting as a means of feeling more in control of their lives and are thrilled to have actually established such incredible self-control. Why should this be any different? Establishing the discipline required to cut gluten from your diet plan can offer you the self-confidence required to take charge of your life in other areas too. Whatever the case might be, delight in the trip. The following chapter is going to assist you in finding out a little bit more about the foods you can eat.

Chapter 8-- So ... What Should You Eat

Do not make the error of presuming that as soon as you change to a gluten-free diet plan, your life is over. Even if you are a food lover, you can still take pleasure in a wide array of tasty and obviously, healthy meals too. All you have to do is modify your point of view.

Rather than looking around and picturing obstacles, take a look at all the brand-new possibilities. This is a chance for you to end up being more selective and more imaginative with your food. Initially, take a cautious look at all the things that you are able to eat with complete confidence that they are gluten-free:

- Unprocessed Seeds (eg. chia, pumpkin and flax seeds).

- Unprocessed Beans

- Raw nuts.

- Veggies.

- A lot of dairy items.

- Eggs.

- Fish.

- Meat.

- Fruits.

- Poultry.

- Gluten-free flours (these could be created from beans, potato, soy, rice, or corn).

- Quinoa

- Hominy corn.

- Millet.

- Tapioca.

- Olive oil.

- Potatoes.

- Ghee.

- Coconut oil.

- Rice.

- Sorghum.

- Teff.

- Soy.

- Wine.

- Cider.

- Port.

- Sherry.

Alternatives to Bread:

- Brown Rice Bread.

- Millet chia bread.

- Ciabatta bread.

- Bhutanese Red Rice Bread.

Alternatives to Pasta:

- Corn Spaghetti.

- Quinoa Pasta.

- Rice-flour penne.

- Spaghetti al Riso.

Although these foods are naturally gluten-free, you still have to be careful. This is specifically so if you have actually not prepped the food yourself. You still have to take notice of just how much calories you take in and just how much fat and sugar you are consuming. Please bear in mind that not everything that is labeled gluten-free is really great for you.

Stay clear of any meat, poultry or fish that has actually been marinated, breaded, coated, or battered. You can never ever be too certain what they included in that combination. It would additionally be a great idea to avoid nuts and legumes that have been processed, and also look at the labels thoroughly prior to consuming them. You can never ever be too sure what was utilized to boost the taste.

Luckily, eating out is still a possibility. Due to all the attention the gluten-free diet plan is getting, numerous gluten-free dining establishments have actually been turning up. Do a fast Google search to determine if there are any in or near your neighborhood. You might even think about launching a business of your own too. Gluten-free dining and even gluten-free support systems are guaranteed to draw in individuals to your facility.

Your gluten-free diet plan is going to impact every part of your life. Please attempt to bear in mind that some medication is going to additionally have gluten too. If you are considering a brand-new physician, make certain to describe that you have actually cut gluten from your diet plan and the explanation for doing so. It additionally goes without stating that you are going to have to look at the labels on your nonprescription drugs really thoroughly too.

Chapter 9-- Simple Gluten-Free Options

Start yourself off with a basic 7-day meal plan. There is no requirement to figure all of it out at the same time. You have time. Consider the foods you currently delight in, determine all the possible sources of gluten, and attempt to remove them. Start simple, and after that, advance from there.

Consider this:

Monday

Meal 1: Scrambled eggs and hash browns

Meal 2: Velvety potato salad with cashews

Meal 3: Ginger and garlic aubergine steak with sweet potato wedges

Tuesday

Meal 1: Gluten-free banana pancakes with agave syrup and blended berry topping

Meal 2: Gluten-free bacon burger

Meal 3: Butter bean stew and meatballs

Wednesday

Meal 1: Breakfast smoothie with fruits of your selection

Meal 2: Sliced BLT salad

Meal 3: Gluten-free chicken pot pie

Thursday

Meal 1: Breakfast hash with sweet potatoes, eggs, and ham

Meal 2: Gluten-free quinoa burger

Meal 3: Cilantro rice and grilled salmon

Friday

Meal 1: Banana berry topping and acai bowl

Meal 2: Gluten-free fish tacos with Mexican cheese and avocado

Meal 3: Gluten-free dumplings and chicken

Saturday

Meal 1: Broccoli and potato frittata

Meal 2: Cheesy chicken chili

Meal 3: Rice noodles and garlic chicken

Sunday

Meal 1: Roasted potato wedges with caramelized onions and tuna

Meal 2: Turkey burger in buns made of zucchini

Meal 3: Shrimp burrito bowl

These dishes consist of things we make at home already. All you have to do is spend some time investigating the gluten-free replacements for the pasta and bread we are used to. Once again, the trick is to keep it enjoyable and to simply keep going.

Consuming a gluten-free diet plan actually does not need to be convoluted. The very best part is that making a meal without gluten does not constantly need to consume a great deal of your valuable time. All you have to do is plan ahead and get some of the prepping finished in advance. Veggies could be sliced up and placed in the fridge for the week. You might even schedule your day of rest for meal prepping and merely reheat your meals as the week continues. There is no requirement to interrupt your regimen. Discover what works for you and stay with it!

Conclusion

My objective was to offer you the most reasonable view of the gluten-free diet plan. Ideally, you ought to have the ability to figure out if the gluten-free diet plan is appropriate for you. What I hope you have actually taken away from this book is that if you do not have a confirmed gluten-associated condition, this might not be the very best diet plan for you. If you are attempting to slim down, there are numerous other options that include minimizing your calorie intake and getting more physical activity. However, if you do choose to continue with this journey, please don't forget to be careful.

If you struggle with celiac disease, gluten sensitivity, or gluten intolerance, I hope you found these recommendations useful. Although the advantages of this diet plan are apparent, I understand that you are going to deal with lots of difficulties. However, there is no embarrassment in requesting assistance. Get your friends and family included. The assistance of your loved ones is going to provide you with the endurance you are going to require to keep going. You might even sign up with a support group. While it is great to have your family applauding you, it would be even better to look for individuals who comprehend what you are undergoing. You might get together personally or perhaps on social networks and share experiences and recipes.

Whether you have Celiac disease or not, you need to continue going. Your health is an extremely crucial matter and you must not take these health problems gently. I do not imply to frighten you, however, a few of the signs connected with these health problems can be deadly. Bear in mind that the primary step to healing is getting your signs examined by a physician.

It is constantly advised to understand simply how major your condition is. There are some circumstances where merely changing your diet plan is not going to suffice. You might additionally require other medications too. Take the suggestions in chapter 4 really seriously due to the fact that these recommendations might make the distinction in whether your physician makes the appropriate medical diagnosis or not.

To conclude, please do not ever feel embarrassed due to your medical diagnosis. Please do not be deceived by all the junk these unethical individuals have labeled as gluten-free. And lastly, please enjoy this brand-new journey regardless of what difficulties you come across.

I hope that you enjoyed reading through this book and that you have found it useful. If you want to share your thoughts on this book, you can do so by leaving a review on the Amazon page. Have a great rest of the day.

Printed in Great Britain
by Amazon